The REAL KAMA SUTRA

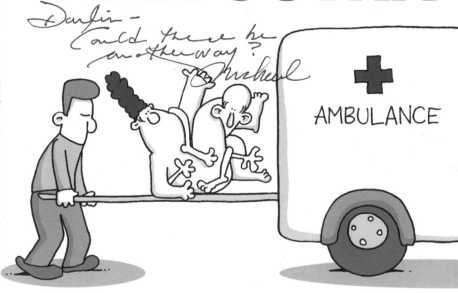

Darlin—
Could there be
another way?
Michael

AMBULANCE

by The Odd Squad

(AND ALLAN PLENDERLEITH)

ℛ
RAVETTE PUBLISHING

First Published by Ravette Publishing Limited 2001
Reprinted 2001, 2002, 2003, 2004, 2005, 2006 (3 times),
2007 (twice), 2008 (twice)

Printed and bound for
Ravette Publishing Limited,
Unit 3, Tristar Centre
Star Road, Partridge Green
West Sussex RH13 8RA

by Gutenberg Press, Malta

ISBN: 978-1-84161-318-5

No. 1
THE 'TURN OFF THE LIGHTS TO HIDE THE FLAB' POSITION.

THE 'QUICK BONK'.

No. 3
THE 'HOW TO <u>REALLY</u> SATISFY A WOMAN IN BED' POSITION.

THE 'TANGLED UP IN SAGGY BOOBS'
POSITION.

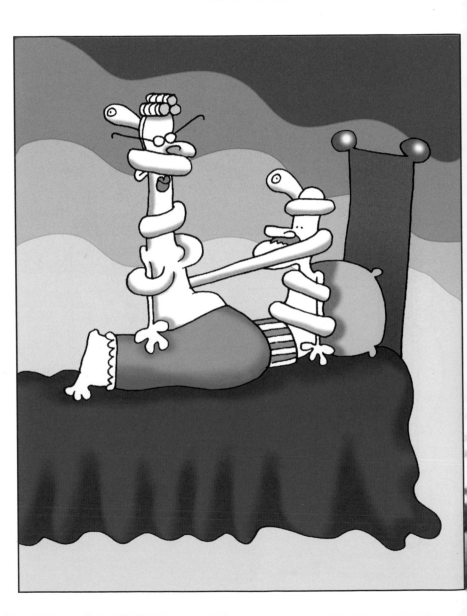

No. 5
THE 'WOMAN GOES ON TOP FOR A CHANGE' POSITION.

No. 6
THE 'SHOULDN'T HAVE HAD THAT CURRY' POSITION.

No. 7
THE 'CAN'T DO IT IF THE DOG'S WATCHING' POSITION.

THE 'MOVE YOUR BUM, I'M TRYING TO WATCH EASTENDERS' POSITION.

THE 'SHOULDN'T HAVE GONE AT IT FOR 9 HOURS LAST NIGHT' POSITION.

THE 'DRANK TOO MUCH AND FELL ASLEEP' POSITION.

No. 11
THE 'SHOULDN'T HAVE LOST THE KEYS TO THE HANDCUFFS' POSITION.

No. 13
THE 'SUSPENDERS SNAP DURING YOUR SEXY DANCE' MOVE.

THE 'TRYING TO CONVINCE THE POLICEMAN THAT THESE ARE ACTUALLY AIRBAGS' POSITION.

THE 'LIGHT UP AFTER SEX' MOVE.

THE 'LET'S NOT WAIT SO LONG UNTIL THE NEXT TIME' POSITION.

THE 'LET'S KEEP THE LIGHT <u>ON</u> DURING SEX' POSITION.

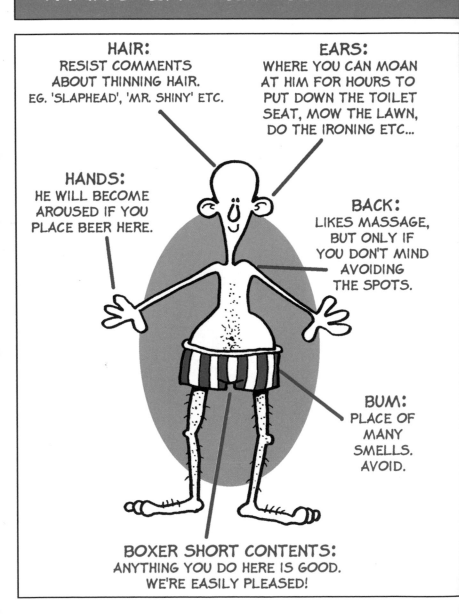

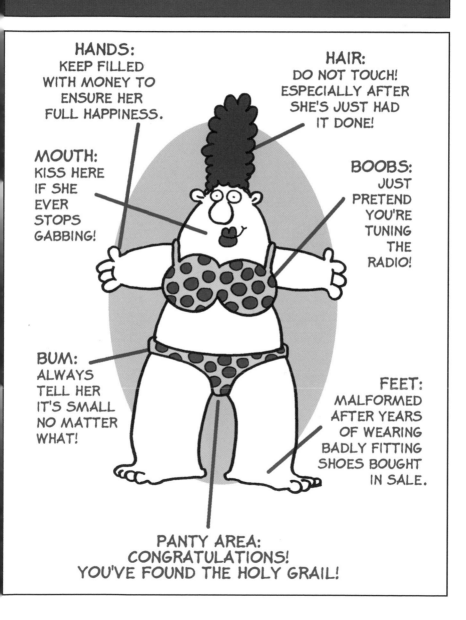

SEX TIP No. 1
NEVER CONFUSE THE ELECTRIC TOOTHBRUSH WITH YOUR VIBRATOR!

SEX TIP No. 2
LADIES – TO ATTRACT MEN, TRY THE NEW PERFUME THAT PROVES IRRESISTIBLE!

SEX TIP No. 3
TO GIVE THE ILLUSION OF AN ACTIVE SEX LIFE, SIMPLY KNOCK HOLES BEHIND YOUR HEADBOARD!

SEX TIP No. 4
MEN – BEWARE OF WOMEN WITH STRONG JAW LINES AND SEE–THROUGH DRESSES!

SEX TIP No. 5
LADIES – IF YOU ASK YOUR MAN TO GIVE YOU A SHINY RING, BE VERY CLEAR WHAT YOU MEAN!

SEX TIP No. 6
NEVER BLOW OFF WHILE DOING IT DOGGY STYLE!

THE PERILS OF HAVING A WOMAN WITH BIG BOOBS.

SEX TIP No. 8
MAKE SURE ALL SEXUAL AIDS ARE REMOVED AFTER USE!

SEX TIP No. 9
MEN – TO SHOW HOW MUCH YOU LOVE HER, TREAT HER TO A SLAP-UP MEAL!

SEX TIP No. 10
NEVER BURP DURING A SNOG!

SEX TIP No. 11
MEN – IF YOU THINK SHE'S READY, SHOW HER YOUR CHOCOLATE STARFISH!

SEX TIP No. 12
IF YOU HAVE DIFFICULTY COMMUNICATING YOUR LOVE, SAY IT WITH FLOWERS!

SEX TIP No. 13
FOR MANY, MAKING A VIDEO OF YOU HAVING SEX IS NOT ACTUALLY A TURN ON.

SEX TIP No. 14
LADIES – IF YOU FIND SEX BORING, JUST LIE BACK AND THINK OF ENGLAND!

SEX TIP No. 15

MEN – IF A GIRL ASKS YOU BACK TO HERS FOR A THREESOME, MAKE SURE YOU ASK EXACTLY WHAT SHE MEANS!

SEX TIP No. 16
OLDER LADIES – BE MORE ROMANTIC BY HIDING GIFTS FOR YOUR LOVED ONE UNDER EACH ROLL OF FLAB!

SEX TIP No. 17
LADIES – IF YOU'RE IN THE MOOD FOR LOVE, TRY GIVING YOUR PARTNER SUBTLE HINTS.

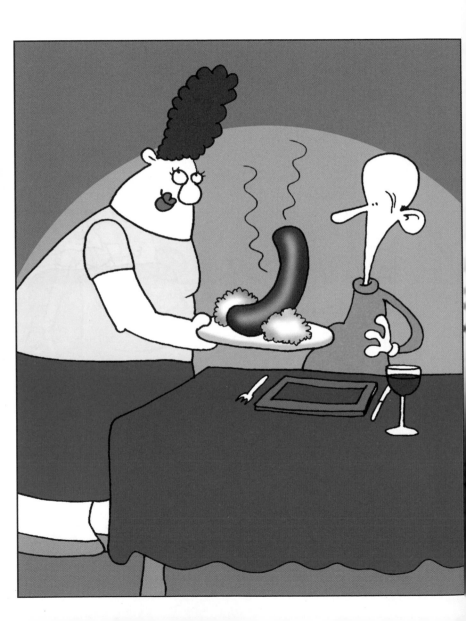

SEX TIP No. 18
IF YOU RUN OUT OF CONDOMS, DON'T WORRY – USE WHATEVER IS TO HAND!

LADIES – TRY NOT TO LET YOUR BOOBS
BOUNCE AROUND SO MUCH DURING SEX.

SEX TIP No. 20
OLDER LADIES – WHY NOT GIVE YOUR MAN A TREAT AND GO WITHOUT A BRA!

SEX TIP No. 21
MEN – REMEMBER TO ALWAYS SPEND HOURS ON FOREPLAY.

SEX TIP No. 22
AVOID SWINGERS PARTIES!

SEX TIP No. 23
LADIES – DO NOT KISS YOUR STUBBLE–FACED MAN WHEN WEARING LOTS OF PERFUME.

SEX TIP No. 24
BE WARNED – SOME WOMEN ARE NOT TRUE BLONDES!

SEX TIP No. 25
IT'S NOT A GOOD IDEA TO SLEEP WITH YOUR HEAD BETWEEN YOUR GIRLFRIEND'S BOOBS.

SEX TIP No. 26
ALWAYS CHECK UNDER THE BED BEFORE YOU BEGIN YOUR PASSIONATE BOUNCING.

SEX TIP No. 27
DURING SEX, MAKE SURE THAT IT DOESN'T SLIP OUT.

SEX TIP No. 28
IF YOU SNEAK HOME FROM WORK TO HAVE A QUICKIE, MAKE SURE YOUR DECOY IS CONVINCING.

SEX TIP No. 29
IF YOU ARE GOING TO SLEEP AROUND, BE PREPARED TO SUFFER THE CONSEQUENCES.

SEX TIP No. 30
MEN – PUT A SOCK DOWN YOUR TRUNKS TO BOOST YOUR MANLY APPEARANCE, JUST MAKE SURE IT DOESN'T SLIP.

SEX TIP No. 31
NEVER HUG TOO HARD IF YOU'VE PUT ON BABY OIL.

SEX TIP No. 32
LADIES – IF YOU COVER YOUR BOYFRIEND IN CHOCOLATE, DON'T GET CARRIED AWAY.

MEN – HOW TO TELL IF YOU'RE
GOOD IN BED!

I. THE NEIGHBOURS COMPLAIN ABOUT THE NOISE!

2. SHE'LL AGREE TO HAVE SEX EVEN IF EASTENDERS IS ON.

PLACES YOU SHOULD HAVE SEX AT LEAST ONCE!

1. IN A FIELD!

2. EVERY ROOM IN YOUR HOUSE!

3. IN YOUR CAR!

4. IN YOUR GARDEN!

5. YOUR MUM + DAD'S BED!

6. A PUBLIC TOILET!

HOW TO SPICE-UP YOUR SEX LIFE!

1. TRY DRESSING UP IN VARIOUS OUTFITS!

2. TRY USING CHOCOLATE SAUCE, STRAWBERRIES AND WHIPPED CREAM!

3. TRY REMOVING YOUR SOCKS BEFORE SEX.

4. WEAR SEXY UNDERWEAR!

5. TRY USING SEX TOYS!

HOW TO STAY SEXY AS YOU GET OLDER!

1. LIVEN UP YOUR ZIMMER FRAME WITH ATTRACTIVE LEOPARD SKIN PRINTS!

2. DON'T LET YOUR TEETH SLIP OUT WHEN YOU'RE SNOGGING!

3. AVOID SUDDEN MOVEMENTS DURING SEX!

4. USE PLENTY OF PERFUME TO MASK THE SMELL OF DECAY!

5. TRIM ALL UNSIGHTLY FACIAL HAIR!

6. CUT SEXY PEEKABOO HOLES IN YOUR INCONTINENCE PANTS!

REASONS WHY SEX IS GOOD FOR YOU!

I. IMPROVES CONCENTRATION – AS YOU TRY TO GET THE CONDOM ON IN THE DARK.

2. IMPROVES EYESIGHT – AS YOU LOOK FOR THE CONDOM THAT FLEW OFF IN THE DARK.

3. BUILDS STOMACH MUSCLES -
WHEN SHE GOES ON TOP.

4. STRENGTHENS SPHINCTER -
AS YOU HOLD IN YOUR
FARTS DURING SEX.

5. IMPROVES BRAIN POWER - AS YOU
FANTASIZE ABOUT SOMEONE
ELSE DURING SEX.

ODD SQUAD titles available...

		ISBN	Price
I Love Beer!	(hardback)	978-1-84161-238-6	£4.99
I Love Dad!	(hardback)	978-1-84161-252-2	£4.99
I Love Mum!	(hardback)	978-1 84161-249-2	£4.99
I Love Poo!	(hardback)	978-1-84161-240-9	£4.99
I Love Sex!	(hardback)	978-1-84161-241-6	£4.99
I Love Wine!	(hardback)	978-1-84161-239-3	£4.99
I Love Xmas!	(hardback)	978-1-84161-262-1	£4.99
The Little Book of Booze		978-1-84161-138-9	£2.99
The Little Book of Men		978-1-84161-093-1	£2.99
The Little Book of Oldies		978-1-84161-139-6	£2.99
The Little Book of Poo		978-1-84161-096-2	£2.99
The Little Book of Pumping		978-1-84161-140-2	£2.50
The Little Book of Sex		978-1-84161-095-5	£2.99
The Little Book of Women		978-1-84161-094-8	£2.99
The Little Book of X-Rated Cartoons		978-1-84161-141-9	£2.99
The Best of Jeff & Maude		978-1-84161-294-2	£9.99
The Odd Squad's Disgusting Book for Boys	(hardback)	978-1-84161-273-7	£7.99
Big Poo Handbook	(hardback)	978-1-84161-168-6	£7.99
Sexy Sex Manual	(hardback)	978-1-84161-220-1	£7.99
I Can Make You Stupid!	(New)	978-1-84161-308-6	£4.99
The Odd Squad Butt Naked		978-1-84161-190-7	£3.99
The Odd Squad Gross Out!		978-1-84161-219-5	£3.99
The Odd Squad Saggy Bits		978-1-84161-218-8	£3.99
The REAL Kama Sutra		978-1-84161-318-5	£4.99
The Odd Squad Volume One		978-1-85304-936-1	£3.99

HOW TO ORDER ... Please send a cheque/postal order in £ sterling, made payable to 'Ravette Publishing' for the cover price of the books and allow the following for postage and packing...

UK & BFPO	70p for the first book & 40p per book thereafter
Europe & Eire	£1.30 for the first book & 70p per book thereafter
Rest of the world	£2.20 for the first book & £1.10 per book thereafter

RAVETTE PUBLISHING   Unit 3, Tristar Centre, Star Road, Partridge Green, West Sussex RH13 8RA

Prices and availability are subject to change without prior notice.